Shrunken Planets

Shrunken
Planets

Robert Louthan

*a*licejamesbooks

Poems in this collection originally appeared in *The Antioch Review, Gargoyle, Green House, Ironwood, Kayak, The New Republic, Partisan Review, Ploughshares, Poetry Now, Seneca Review,* and *Slow Loris Reader.*

The publication of this book was assisted by a grant from the Massachusetts Council for the Arts and Humanities.

Library of Congress Catalogue Card Number 79-54883
ISBN 0-914086-28-6
Printed in the United States of America
Typeset by Jeffrey Schwartz
Designed by Audrey Sichel

Grateful acknowledgment is made to Harper & Row, Publishers, Inc., for the lines on page vi from *Amen* by Yehuda Amichai, translated from the Hebrew by the author and Ted Hughes. Copyright © 1977 by Yehuda Amichai.

ALICE JAMES BOOKS
138 Mt. Auburn Street
Cambridge, Massachusetts 02138

For My Mother
And For Sue Owen

To live is to build a ship and a harbor
at the same time. And to complete the harbor
long after the ship was drowned.
                            Yehuda Amichai

Contents

1

2   The Diary

3

4

5

1

for Alan Nagel

You lift the violin so carefully, as if
it is the larynx from an extinct animal.
The audience quiets down. You think

of the musician who wept blood when
a string snapped and threaded his eye.
The instrument feels your chin

in the palm of its fingerless hand.
Now you play so well that,
as each note dies, the next one

inherits. You barely hear the bow
catch its breath to change direction,
or the last note, buried alive in applause.

Kids Are Young

If a tremendous tear takes over your train set
and the history of your hands comes back from the
      beach,
don't sulk, don't put the weekend in your mother's
      purse,
don't think from scratch;

if your father sings to you from a busy intersection in his
      voice
and the shadows of the blind appear,
don't pick a playmate who works in the past
or an orange with vacationing seeds, don't disgust a
      toothbrush.

Be brave, little child.

The bread baked in the shape of an ambulance
drives through dinner, looking for a place to park
in your appetite.

Each thing has its place, and the place
doesn't complain. The wound, though unable
to live with it, holds the scab.

The oyster keeps the pearl like a promise.
The lamp is willing to sweat things out
when light is born in its bulb.

The Shoes

Whenever I took off my shoes
I undid the laces like stitches,
but they hadn't healed.
I should have known it was hopeless.

Once I was so tired, I told them
to take a walk on their own.
They stole a bicycle
and pedaled it into the river.

Now I gladly go barefoot.
Someday, I'll pull one of them up
with a fishing pole, regret
that its tongue has tasted the bait.

The way I see things asks for a room of its own.
And I have other regrets, too: the remains
of exploded stuffed animals, an educational toy
with blackmail in mind, and the past, which
threatens to throw out my childhood. Still I
have hope, though my chances avoid me like stars,
though I consider suicide, a slight possibility
that works out with weights in my sleep.

Yes, the way I see things asks for a room
of its own. I say no and, in a temper tantrum,
it disfigures the furniture. I must find
a new way to see things, a way that leads
to the origins they contain and introduces me.
Then I may find that I share a self. The animals,
the toy, the past through whose heart
my childhood flows, they think I'm blind.

Children change
when a toy touches them.
They look into each other's eyes
to see the bullets at the back
of those barrels.

Then they let the toy rust in rain.
Years later, they exclude it
from letters written to one another,
envelopes that postmen vacuum-pack
into remote mailboxes.

Each synapse like a blown fuse,
I can't meditate any more;
what meant too much to me
is no longer carried by current.
What was it? Perhaps nothing:
a miniature moon,
dissolved in my mouth.

I've Always Been A Matador

Really, beloved audience,
those ivory gloves you applaud with
are cracking to pieces.
The bull, closer to me than an hour,
is dead. I throw you his ear,
which is severed and listening.

2

The Diary

My reflection peeled from the mirror, exposing a gray silhouette. As I touched this, dry stains were left on the tips of my fingers. The reflection had fallen to the floor. Picking it up, I felt its papery texture. I turned it around. The back was transparent. I reversed it again and pressed it into place on the mirror. It didn't hold.

I put glue on the back. This time, the reflection stayed on the mirror. There were lumps where the glue wasn't evenly spread. I tried to smooth them out. It got torn. I left it like that.

I went and washed my hands. The stains wouldn't come off. I dried them and put a pair of gloves on.

I returned to the mirror. Nothing was visible in it. I switched some lights on. No matter how many I used, the mirror remained totally dark. Without removing my gloves, I felt the surface. It was flat again.

Everything I touch now is with these gloves on.

On the street, I noticed a small boy following me. His head was completely covered by a bandage. I stopped walking and waited for him to catch up. He was holding a sheet of sandpaper, and asked me the time. As I spoke to him, the bandage burst into flames.

I had a dream:

I was an old man. My mother, dead at that point, was preparing food. I walked into the kitchen. She said, "Your father won't be home for supper. So, if you wish, you may wear prosthetic hands to the table. There's a pair on the shelf of the hall closet." I brought them into the kitchen and tried to put them on. "Your own hands have to be removed first," said my mother. She picked up a steak knife and told me to place one of my hands on the cutting board. I did, without taking my gloves off. She dug the knife into my arm just above where the glove ended.

"That hurts," I said.

After cutting off both my hands, my mother carried them in their gloves to the hall closet. She put them on the shelf and shut the door. Back in the kitchen, she attached the mechanical hands to my stumps. They fit perfectly. As we sat down to eat, my father walked in.

I was traveling by train. The conductor came to me and said, "We had to remove the wheels from this train years ago; they were too dark. We've been riding without wheels ever since. If you want, we can go back for them. You are in love with the week in which they are kept."

I said, "No, I don't want to."

I found a statue of myself in the park. He was carved in wood and his hands were stained. For the first time, I removed my gloves. The tips of my fingers were clean. I put the gloves on his hands. They fit perfectly.

No one has ever been so young as I have just become.

3

Elegy For My Father

Doniphan Louthan, 1920-1952

I do not remember the day you disappeared.
I was too young to understand,
still small enough to curl up in your hat.
When I questioned mother
years later, she told me you had gone
to heaven, but I knew better.
You were in her heart, and kept it beating
by pacing back and forth.

The Signal

for Michael Ryan

When my father found out
he didn't have long to live,
he carved a whistle of bone
from himself, and dried a ball
of blood in it. Handing it
to me, he said, "If you use this,
I'll come back." He died just then.
I've often touched the whistle
to my lips, with my breath held.

Each night I pray
to *a steel box with a hole in it*
from which an eye observes.
I hold it, heavier than sleep,
in my hands, while it watches my face
sweat solid, miniature seagulls.
I ask the eye to contain me
like a ship in a bottle.
But if it does, the box will go blind.

I Try To Call It

Disturbed, as if I'd brought
a mismatched pair of lungs back
from the laundromat, or the alarm
in my heart had gone off early,

as if just anything had happened
when I'd expected the specific,
I swallow a stone and digest it.
The calmness of statues

comes over me. My eyes sit
on their tears, but none hatches.
My name, when I try to call it,
dissolves on the tip of my tongue.

As a child, I built
a sand castle for my brother,
who'd drowned. While the tide
took it to him, hope, delicate
as a lightbulb filament,
burned and broke in my brain.

I still walk that beach,
which, like a decision,
is reached by waves,
but they back down.

As a child, I took a radio apart
to see who was singing. It was still
plugged in, so I got these electrical burns
on my hands, a type of tattoo
not even drunks would want to wear.

Most people I meet try not to be
touched, as if what hurt my hands
is contagious, or as if the reason
the skin isn't smooth is that
I haven't washed it in weeks.

But one woman insists I slip both hands
inside her, so she's put through
the pain that preceded the scars.
My fingers come out basted with blood.

Then she sings like she did on the radio.

While my wife kisses my neck
on our wedding night
I crack my knuckles, then
hold her. Nine months from now,
a child we won't know
will be born. We'll know the name
of who we want him to become.
When he wakes us, we'll lift him
from his crib to the window,
under the sky dyed black
and the starched moon. I look
at the crucifix on the wall.
Please, god, don't let him be you.

I Hug Myself Hard

I dream my lungs
are converted to wasp nests.
The doctor said there's no cure
for cancer. I can't
cough the insects out.

At breakfast I tell my wife
the dream and that
I should have stopped smoking
before it broke my body.
Touching my hand, she says
but you weren't wise enough.

No. Then we dress,
she drives me to the hospital.
Beside her in the car
the pain returns so I hug myself
hard. It doesn't help and I like it.

The hospital hardens around me
like a scab. The more I scratch it,
the worse it gets. The doctor tries
to persuade me to speak, his stethoscope
at my lips like a magnet. "The lungs
are the wings of the voice," he says.
"They beat against a sky inside them."
He translates a letter I receive
from my shadow: "You've had a streak
of bad luck. You must learn to roll
doubles with your eyes, see the full moon,
that coin the night saves just for you,
placed in the plate of the window."

The Suicide

By the positions of starfish,
I navigate the course of my drowning.
Soon asleep, I dream of that boat left above
without a name or wooden anchor.

1

Not just anyone can talk, even
to himself, the way he wants.
Open my larynx when I die.
You'll find the fossil
of a word I haven't said.

2

Fill my lungs with melted metal
to cast, in those molds,
a pair of something extinct.

The Weather Here

for Heather McHugh

When the tough get going, I'm left here alone
in this limited part of the planet.
They write that their new addresses are better,

that I wouldn't think so, and that all is well
with me. O I want to believe them, there's
no sense in relying on first-hand experience

now that I take drugs strong enough to relax
a building. I don't want to look at
the bracelet of scars I started, and boy was I

disappointed that the blood didn't come up blue
like it is under my skin. The weather here
is nice, final. I have some plans, but they're small.

On nights when the moon matters,
its light, like an inspiration,
demands that I look out the window.

And on one such night I see
a woman in the yard. She calls to me,
asking if a kiss has lips.

Soon, even our nakedness hangs
on my bedpost, as we search each other
for a permanent orgasm.

To Make It Better

I take my heart out for repairs
and show my wife the hole in my chest.
Before I can stop her, she kisses the wound

to make it better. She is proud of her work,
will not forgive me if I undo it
to put the muscle back in.

I spend the car loan on a grand piano, which I park in the living room. When my wife complains, I say, "But, Honey, you wouldn't want a Buick in here, would you?"

I work under the hood, giving it a tune-up, then ask my wife to sit beside me on the seat. I read the sheet music in front of me like a map. With my feet on the accelerator, clutch, and brake pedals, I drive the piano through a composition.

At the end of our trip, she says, "I'd rather have a Buick. This thing doesn't even come with a radio."

Remembering that marriage is made of compromise, I install a radio in the piano.

The Divorce

My wife lifts the lids
of her eye sockets, empty
except for the masturbating
spiders. I turn away.
"You don't love me," she says

and chews on her voice until
only its skeleton remains.
We take off our wedding rings,
each set with half
of the same shrunken planet.

The world is worse, you say,
than your difficult dreams.
And so you sleep
while cars curve by
on the way to work, while
sunlight leaks onto your lawn.
You dream that your bed
has only one side
for you to get up on,
that your wife, since she died,
gets up on the other,
and that you wake at noon
with nothing in the window
worth knowing, not even
your faint reflection, which
asks you why the dream comes true.

Jealousy complies with some of us. One of us is the man whose wife is a sleeper. Each evening she makes an excuse: "I am tired," she will say, or "It is late." He knows that she is digging a tunnel in her sleep, nightly extending it toward a field, where she will surface in mist.

Himself a faithful man, he lies awake beside her; and often his jealousy comes to the door, checking to see that he is not filling with sleep.

One night, to pass the time, he imagines that he too is a sleeper. He turns on the bedside lamp and makes sketches of possible dreams. His jealousy opens the door, and this time walks in, confessing a weakness for art. They agree that one sketch is particularly striking: his wife is depicted as having finished her tunnel and made her way to a field. She is gathering mist onto a stone: his face. He knows that this is the perfect guess.

When she wakes up, he hands her the sketch. "Now," she says, "you can share what I must suffer."

O to inherit the kiss that began your family!
Through this night held down by hibernating
     constellations,
I carry an arrow plucked from the Great Bear.
The arrowhead is sharp as a candleflame, and my
     thoughts,
its chorus of simile, rise from the street
like parking meters, gleaming. I stop
at each one, insert a coin engraved with your face.

How We Become Closer

It's too hot tonight to cook.
When we open the window
a cube of the outside slides in
and stops, suspended above
the floor. Reaching over it
we shut the window.
The transparent black cube
and the bushtop enclosed in it
fall and shatter. We put
the smallest pieces
on our plates. The silverware
has sunk into the table.
Only the handles protrude,
impossible to pull.

You've learned to live
in a house that has nothing
outside, each windowpane
replaced with a photograph
of the section of landscape
that used to appear in it
from behind. Because
the perspective won't change
if you walk toward the wall,
you just lie in bed. How
simple this is.
It's always day in your house,
which the dark you don't see
surrounds. You think
of when the world was real:
the woman you wanted woke
beside you, touched your arm,
then scrambled eggs into sunlight
in the kitchen. You stare
at the window, see
the photographed back of her body,
bent by overstuffed suitcases
she holds, in the distance.

Prelude To Masturbation

You receive a kiss in your sleep.
Waking, you are surprised to find you have it.
"A kiss is buried inside me," you say.
Now you must make many visits
to your body, place a wreath of fingers
on that extravagant grave.

My woman speaks to me
in kiss language. She says
love, with an accent
that helps my whole body
hear. Love in my name, love
in my heart made of lipstick.
And she smells my soul,
that daisy, destroyed
by she loves me loves me
not. She puts the petals
back on! Today it's intense
to be the man from myself.

Sometimes I'm so lonely,
I want to break into the mirror
and visit my double.
Only an embrace
could convince me I live.

Up before dawn,
I leave you alone on the bed
to continue your search
for a furnished dream. I look out
at the stars abandoned above
this street haunted by its own dead end,
at the car that we will wake
within an hour, a monument parked
in front of the motel. I don't
recognize us now, though the luggage
knows our initials, each the head
of a decapitated name,
and contains the clothes we've tried
to become. Maybe it matters
where we've been, or will drive
when the sun starts baking its daily bread
in the clouds, but I wouldn't care
even if we could say.
I'll hold you until someday
we turn into statues, but now I just want
your eyes to open, and see me
standing here, no one, next to you.

Woman of enameled distances, of lunar assembly lines,
of elastic silence, woman of the orchestral diaphragm
and disposable comma,
woman of adult fire, of the acoustic hairbrush, woman of
hourly days and cubic desire,
woman of possible women,

I want to oil at once the gear that propels your caress,
to upholster the bones of the dead if it helps you to think
in duplicate,
to guess from the length of your glance your secret
handkerchief, your independent dinette, and
hung-over library;

I want, without courthouses or anesthesia, to sort out the
riveted luncheons that famine constructs,
to find on the map your molecular minute,
your mahogany eyelashes, the screw that tightens in
your nostalgia.

I speak to you now with the voice of martyred bees,
hoping to drown out my echoing tricycle,
my luminous pencils of ambition, my afternoon laced
with preservatives.

From a boudoir ruled by arthritic mirrors,
in prosthetic darkness, through a collision of portable
neighborhoods
to startled heights placed on pedestals,
I escort a severe checkerboard, a professional bandage,
and propose a toast of ink to your athletic ribcage and
mood.

5

If the chessmen looked
approachable, I'd take a survey:
Do you have faith
in your king and queen.
Are you a determinist. What
about the possibility of peace.

Can any even think.
Now we're getting somewhere.
Whoever doesn't want his hand
amputated, raise it.

No piece on the board
owns good property.
When killed, they can't be buried
and must leave that flat planet.

Nothing Else

A poet writes about writing only when he can think of nothing else. Anonymous

I throw myself into my work
like a wave onto the beach.
It absorbs me; I forget the buoys
I've shouldered and left stranded.
Nothing can pull me away but the moon,

that ball bearing that made the earth
run smoothly until it fell out,
whose reflection in water rotates
to turn the tide on what now
is littered with clams for you.

I always hated gym class.
We put on jockstraps, those holsters
hidden under our uniforms, took

painful injections of pushups,
and passed a ball around
like a counterfeit planet.

Then we suffered the weather
in the shower room. Each of us
had his separate storm.

Beside you on the beach
a wrecked rowboat, with oars
in tattered gloves of seaweed,
sprouts leaves, swallows light.

Three-dimensional mirrors,
flexible and shaped like gulls,
pull the ocean into waves
with their webbed feet, let
go, then spin fast enough
to wear away, hollow,
each releasing a real gull.

The fishing rod vibrates
in your hand. The punctured worm,
now loose, dripping wet, creeps
toward you along the line.

The Best Poem Ever Written

for Donald Hall

It's guaranteed to change you,
or I will personally die. Sit back
and relax while it makes history
in your most private decades.
Believe in it when there's nothing.

Amaze your friends by bringing it up
during physical conversations
about love. It's better than sleep.
If you buy it now, more of your
subjective stars will work. Own it.

Reproductions of this unsigned painting hang in every home. The style, impressive enough to compensate for the lack of a permanent subject matter, must be what makes the work a popular success.

The critics are withholding judgment until they're shown the original. They object to the fact that the copies aren't uniform, though they see themselves in each one and wonder if this is a bribe.

He always filled his prayers
with fresh numerals.
Unsure where energy goes
in sex, he watched his wife
sort things out there.

When a microscope showed him
the open grave in an atom,
he knew his was a life
of which only the end works.
The clock close by
as he slept still shivers.

The Beggar

The beggar takes
his face off
like a mask
and holds it out,
hollow side up,
in his hand.

Where the face was,
his skull now shines
in the severe
sunlight,
his eyes still in
their sockets.

He watches a stranger
come by. Her tears,
wept for him,
fall into the face.
He puts it back on.
He can use them.

These shut-ins share the sanitarium
of my closet, each crippled
to nothing but shoulders

and the essential part of the head:
a question mark to hang on with.
All I can do for them

is break their clothes in.
Taking a shirt, I strip one naked,
pretend my touch is by accident.

When the insane see
the full moon's ton of light
in the window, they stay up all night
like clocks, the alarms inside them
set to go off. They look for
lipstick marks on clouds,
paint each other's eyes out
as their suits come back conscious
from the cleaners.

A man walking. The sun is up,
the sky around it dark as night.
His shadow, made of light,
illuminates the road
in front of him. Solid snowflakes
have fallen. Those in his footprints
are bent and broken.
On his cheeks, tiny loaves of bread
shaped like tears. And in his hand,
a red neon chain leash
attached to his tight collar.

You are born with the seed of a wound
in each hand. And over your head,
a zero of light. This is the life.
It will end when what you build with wood
crosses you out behind your back.

Too old to carry your easel
any more, you stop to set it up
in a field, and prepare the paints
for your last landscape.
Each detail, as you copy it now,
disappears from your subject.
When you finish,
what you've painted on the canvas
has been replaced beyond it
by a black square. You view the picture
from the perspective
in which it fits that square.
By not looking away, you live forever.

Robert Louthan was born in 1951 and raised on Long Island, New York. He was educated at Empire State College (B.A., 1976) and Goddard College (M.F.A., 1978). In 1978, he was awarded the Grolier Poetry Prize and a *Transatlantic Review* scholarship to the Bread Loaf Writers' Conference. He lives in Cambridge, Massachusetts.